U.S. Department of Justice
Office of Justice Programs
National Institute of Justice

I0448712

NIJ

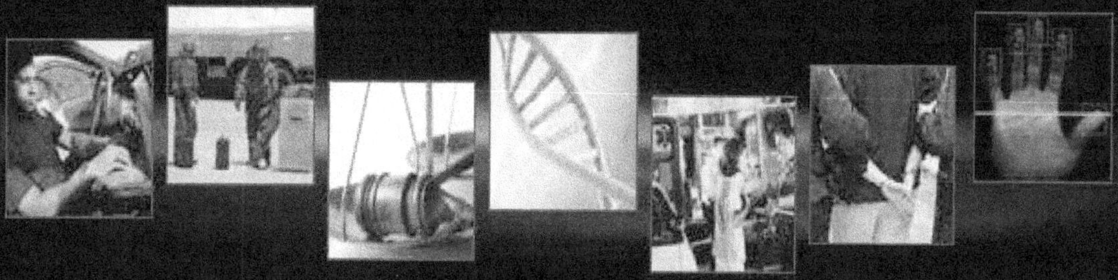

HIGH-PRIORITY CRIMINAL JUSTICE
TECHNOLOGY NEEDS

2010

U.S. Department of Justice

Office of Justice Programs

810 Seventh Street N.W.

Washington, DC 20531

Eric H. Holder, Jr.
Attorney General

Laurie O. Robinson
Assistant Attorney General

John H. Laub
Director, National Institute of Justice

This and other publications and products of the
National Institute of Justice can be found at:

National Institute of Justice
www.ojp.usdoj.gov/nij

Office of Justice Programs
Innovation • Partnerships • Safer Neighborhoods
www.ojp.usdoj.gov

July 2010
NCJ 230391

Table of Contents

NIJ's Mission and Organization

As the research, development and evaluation arm of the U.S. Department of Justice, the Office of Justice Programs' National Institute of Justice (NIJ) is dedicated to researching crime control and justice issues to help enhance the criminal justice system and increase public safety.

NIJ provides objective, independent evidence-based knowledge and tools to meet the challenges of crime and justice, particularly at the state and local levels. NIJ's diverse audience includes:

- Policymakers at all levels of government.
- Practitioners who work in the criminal justice field.
- Researchers.
- The American public.

The Director of NIJ, who is appointed by the President and confirmed by the Senate,

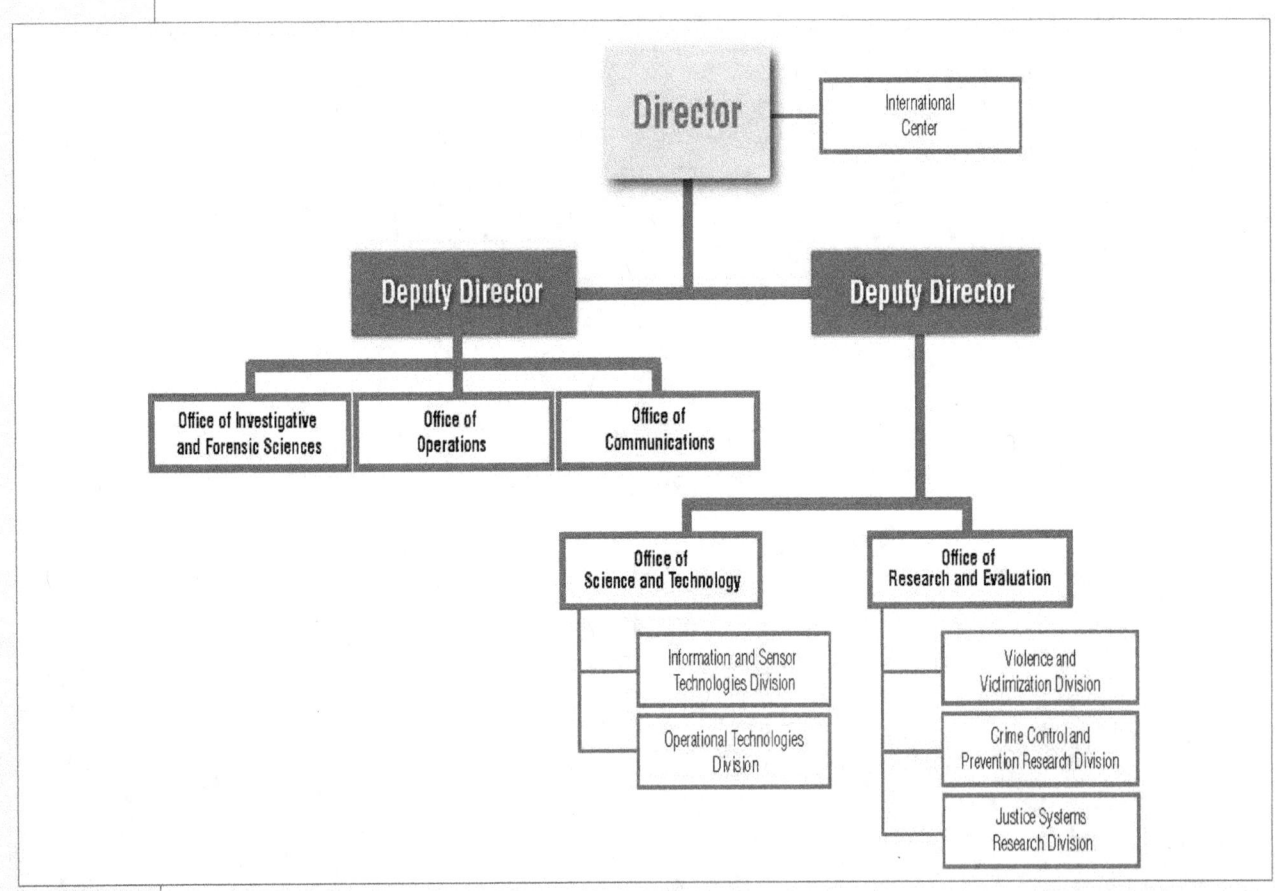

NIJ organizational structure chart.

establishes the Institute's objectives in light of those of the U.S. Department of Justice and its Office of Justice Programs. When setting policy and practice, NIJ actively solicits the views of criminal justice and other professionals and researchers.

NIJ's organizational structure is designed to integrate the social and physical sciences to maximize cross-discipline research, development and evaluation. New tools and technologies are not in themselves solutions without appropriate policies and practices. Policies and practices must effectively integrate technology.

NIJ has five offices:

■ The Office of Research and Evaluation, which develops, conducts, directs and supervises social science research and evaluation activities across a wide variety of criminal justice issues. Its activities include evaluation research on how well tools and technologies meet the needs of the field.

■ The Office of Science and Technology, which manages technology research, development, testing and evaluation; the development of guides and technical standards; compliance testing; and programs to build capacity and provide technology assistance to local, state and, as appropriate, tribal and federal law enforcement, corrections and court agencies, and crime laboratories.

■ The Office of Investigative and Forensic Sciences, which is involved in research to improve the quality and practice of the forensic sciences, in investigative and forensic technology research and development, and in programs to enhance the capacity of the investigative and forensic components of the criminal justice system.

■ The Office of Communications, which plays a key role in NIJ's efforts to move research findings into evidence-based policy and practice. It disseminates the results of NIJ research through an integrated publishing, conferencing, marketing and outreach strategy.

■ The Office of Operations, which manages the business and administrative processes necessary to NIJ conducting its mission.

NIJ also has an International Center. It is involved in research on international criminal activities that have a domestic effect. It is also involved in research and evaluation of the criminal justice policies and practices of other countries that may be useful in meeting the challenges of crime and justice in the United States.

NIJ's principal authorities are derived from the Omnibus Crime Control and Safe Streets Act of 1968, as amended (see 42 USC § 3721-3723), and, as it relates to the activities of its Office of Science and Technology, from Title II of the Homeland Security Act of 2002.

NIJ's Office of Science and Technology

Criminal justice practitioners, such as law enforcement and corrections officers, increasingly rely on technology to do their jobs. Through its Office of Science and Technology, NIJ (1) serves as the national focal point for work on criminal justice technology; and (2) carries out programs that, by providing equipment, training and technical assistance, improve the safety and effectiveness of criminal justice technology as well as access to that technology by local, state, tribal and federal enforcement agencies. The Office of Science and Technology's principal tasks in supporting this mission include:

- Establishing and maintaining advisory groups to assess the technology needs of state, local, tribal and federal criminal justice agencies.

- Establishing and maintaining performance standards for criminal justice tools and technologies.

- Establishing and conducting a compliance-testing program to ensure that the tools and technologies used by criminal justice agencies are safe and effective.

- Carrying out a research, development, testing and evaluation (RDT&E) program to improve the safety and effectiveness of criminal justice technology.

- Providing technical assistance to criminal justice practitioners.

- Serving as a clearinghouse for information on criminal justice technologies.

The Office of Science and Technology also operates the National Law Enforcement and Corrections Technology Center (NLECTC) system. Created in 1994, the NLECTC system plays a vital role in enabling the Office of Science and Technology to carry out its mission. The NLECTC system's centers and offices provide:

- Scientific and technical support to NIJ's RDT&E projects, particularly the identification of criminal justice technology needs.

- Support for the transfer and adoption of technology into practice by law enforcement and corrections agencies, criminal justice courts agencies and crime laboratories.

- Assistance in developing and disseminating technology guidelines and standards.

- Technology assistance, information and support to law enforcement and corrections agencies, courts and crime laboratories.

The Office of Science and Technology manages the NLECTC system as a whole and the individual centers within it, except for the Forensic Sciences Technology Center of Excellence, which is managed by the Office of Investigative and Forensic Sciences.

National Law Enforcement and Corrections Technology Center System

One office and three types of centers comprise the NLECTC system. These are:

- The Office of Law Enforcement Standards, which is a component of the Department of Commerce's National Institute of Standards and Technology.

- The National Center.

- The Technology Centers of Excellence.

- The Regional Centers.

All of these components work together as part of an integrated NLECTC system.

The Office of Law Enforcement Standards assists NIJ to develop performance standards.

The National Center serves as the technology information clearinghouse of the NLECTC system. It also administers NIJ's equipment Compliance-Testing Program.

The Technology Centers of Excellence are the authoritative resource within the NLECTC system

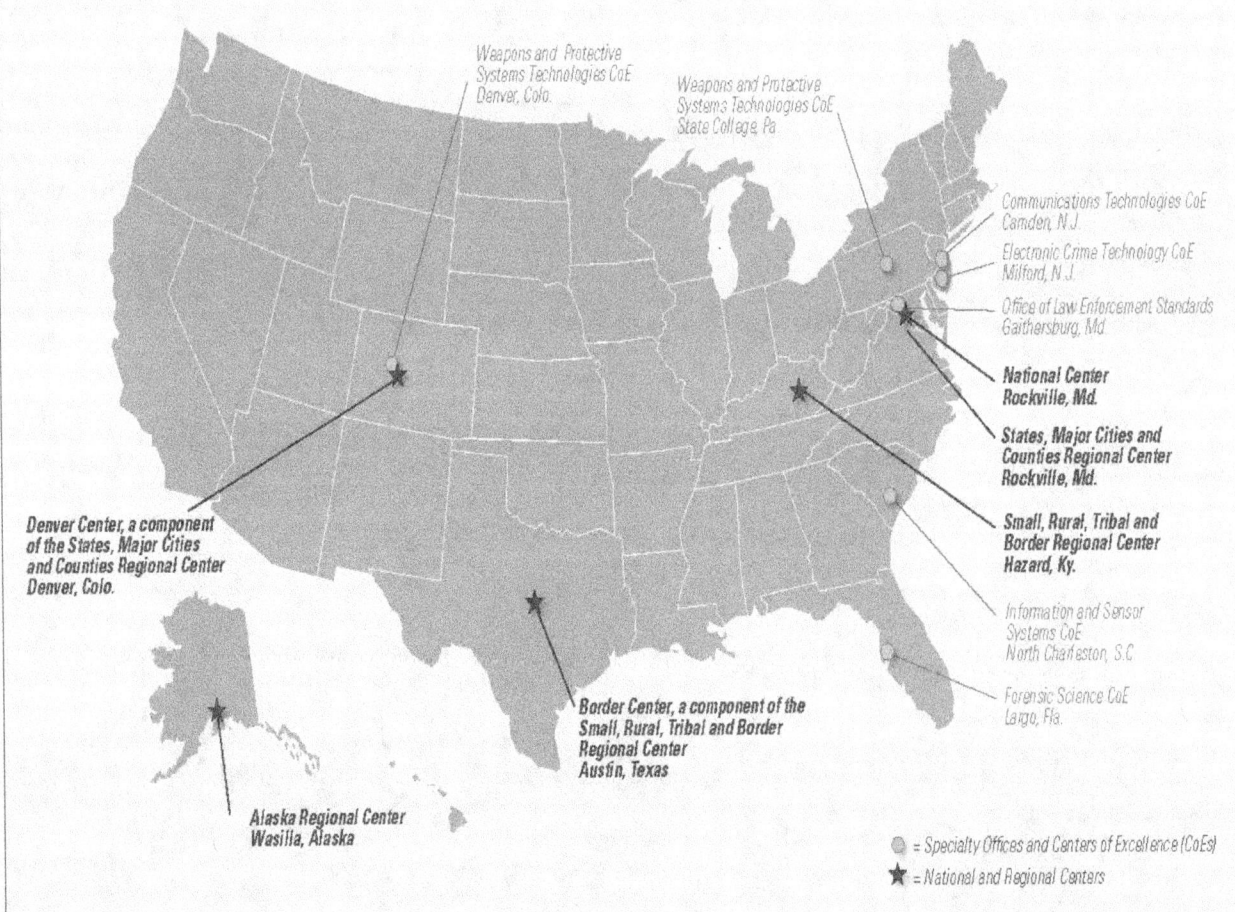

Weapons and Protective Systems Technologies CoE Denver, Colo.

Weapons and Protective Systems Technologies CoE State College, Pa.

Communications Technologies CoE Camden, N.J.

Electronic Crime Technology CoE Milford, N.J.

Office of Law Enforcement Standards Gaithersburg, Md.

National Center Rockville, Md.

States, Major Cities and Counties Regional Center Rockville, Md.

Small, Rural, Tribal and Border Regional Center Hazard, Ky.

Information and Sensor Systems CoE North Charleston, S.C.

Forensic Science CoE Largo, Fla.

Denver Center, a component of the States, Major Cities and Counties Regional Center Denver, Colo.

Border Center, a component of the Small, Rural, Tribal and Border Regional Center Austin, Texas

Alaska Regional Center Wasilla, Alaska

⬤ = Specialty Offices and Centers of Excellence (CoEs)

★ = National and Regional Centers

National Law Enforcement and Corrections Technology Center System (cont.)

for practitioners and developers in their technology area(s) of focus. Their primary role is to assist in the transition of technology from the laboratory into practice. They accomplish this mainly through activities related to the testing, evaluation and demonstration of new technologies and through provision of technology assistance to first adopting agencies. Each Center of Excellence supports one or more of NIJ's technology investment portfolios. A list of these portfolios can be found on page 10.

The Regional Centers are the initial point of entry for practitioners to the NLECTC system and provide generalized technology assistance to agencies within their regions. As needed, they forward requests for specialized assistance to the appropriate Center of Excellence. They also support the Centers of Excellence in coordinating technology demonstrations and evaluations with agencies within their regions.

NIJ's Office of Investigative and Forensic Sciences

The Office of Investigative and Forensic Sciences (OIFS) is the federal government's lead agency for forensic science research and development as well as the administration of programs that facilitate training and improve laboratory efficiency. OIFS was part of the Office of Science and Technology until 2009, when the division was elevated to a separate office within the Institute to highlight the importance of the forensic sciences. OIFS programs provide direct support to crime laboratories and law enforcement agencies to increase their capacity to process high-volume cases, provide needed training in new technologies, and provide support to reduce backlogs through the DNA Initiative, the Coverdell Forensic Science Improvement Grants Program, the Solving Cold Cases With DNA Program and the Forensic Science Training Development and Delivery Program. With highly qualified personnel and strong ties to the community, OIFS plays a leadership role in directing efforts to address the needs of our nation's forensic science community.

The Office of Investigative and Forensic Sciences' research and development efforts focus on three primary goals. These are:

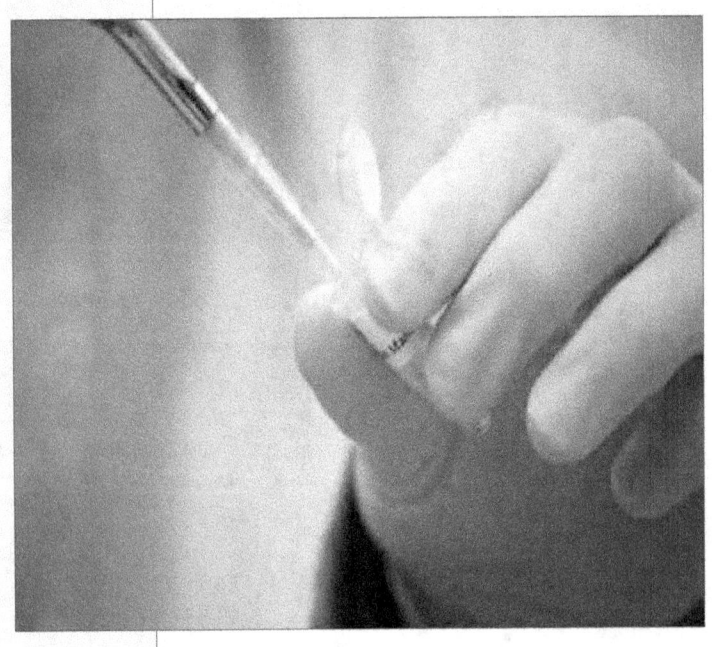

- To expand the information that can be extracted from traditional types of forensic evidence, including DNA, and quantify its evidentiary value.

- To develop reliable and widely applicable tools and technologies that allow faster, cheaper and less labor-intensive identification, collection, preservation and analysis of forensic evidence of all kinds and reduce existing case backlogs.

- To establish the scientific basis of the forensic science disciplines.

NIJ's Office of Research and Evaluation

The Office of Research and Evaluation plays an integral part in NIJ's efforts to address the technology needs of the criminal justice community. Evaluation research establishes the efficacy of a new tool or technology, and informs the development of optimum policies and practices.

One of the most important aspects of managing a criminal justice program or developing a new tool or technology is ensuring that the program or technology is meeting its goals and objectives. An evaluation is the best way to accomplish that. An evaluation not only produces evidence about how a program or technology works (or does not) but it also shows us where to adjust and fine-tune so the program or technology has the greatest impact.

The Office of Research and Evaluation's technology evaluation efforts involve both technologies that are well established in practice as well as new technology.

Predictive Policing Pilot Program

In 2009, NIJ's Office of Science and Technology and Office of Research and Evaluation initiated a joint effort to explore the potential of information and geospatial technology, coupled with innovative interventions, to reduce crime and improve public safety. This concept has been given a working title of "predictive policing."

Predictive policing proposes that law enforcement agencies use data analysis to inform their policing strategies in much the same way that businesses use it to anticipate market conditions or industry trends and to drive sales strategies. The concept involves taking data from disparate sources, analyzing it and then using that information to anticipate, prevent and respond more effectively to future crime.

Predictive policing borrows from well-established policing techniques, such as community-oriented policing. It is not meant to replace, but rather to enhance, these techniques by providing a framework to help better organize policing as an information-intensive business in an information age.

In 2009, NIJ made awards to seven jurisdictions to implement pilot programs to evaluate the efficacy of the concept. Awards were made to the Boston, Chicago, New York City and Washington Metropolitan police departments as well as the Los Angeles Police Foundation, the Maryland State Police and the Shreveport (La.) Police Department. A separate award was made to the RAND Corporation to provide analytical and research support to this effort in general, and to those agencies in particular.

The pilot programs are expected to continue through fiscal year 2014.

How NIJ Sets Its Technology Research Agenda

The needs of criminal justice practitioners in the field drive NIJ's research, development, testing and evaluation (RDT&E) agenda.

Two specialized entities play an important role in advising its RDT&E investments: Technology Working Groups and the Law Enforcement and Corrections Technology Advisory Council.

Technology Working Groups (TWGs). A TWG is a practitioner-based committee of approximately 20 experienced individuals drawn from local, state, tribal and federal criminal justice agencies and laboratories. NIJ's science and technology program is organized around technology investment portfolios. Each portfolio has a TWG associated with it. TWG members have expertise relevant to the particular portfolio with which their TWG is associated. TWGs are hosted by the NLECTC system Center of Excellence that supports that portfolio.

The TWGs, and through them the criminal justice practitioner community, are embedded in the NIJ RDT&E process from beginning to end. The main purpose of a TWG is to identify the criminal justice technology needs within a given portfolio. TWG members also participate in the peer-review panels that evaluate potential solutions to address those needs. Further, the agencies from which TWG members are

---

NIJ's Technology Investment Portfolios

- Aviation.

- Biometrics.

- Body Armor.

- Communications.

- Community Corrections.

- DNA Forensics.

- Electronic Crime.

- Explosive Device Defeat.

- General (non-DNA) Forensics.

- Geospatial Technologies.

- Information-Led Policing and Courts Technologies.

- Institutional Corrections.

- Less-Lethal Technologies.

- Operations Research/Modeling and Simulation.

- Officer Safety and Protective Technologies.

- Pursuit Management.

- School Safety.

- Sensors and Surveillance.

drawn are routinely involved in the testing and evaluation of the resulting solutions.

Law Enforcement and Corrections Technology Advisory Council (LECTAC). LECTAC is made up of senior criminal justice practitioners from law enforcement, corrections and courts agencies, and crime laboratories. LECTAC reviews the recommendations of the TWGs annually and advises NIJ on prioritizing investments across its technology portfolios from a criminal justice agency, senior management perspective. LECTAC is hosted by the NLECTC system National Center.

In developing its annual assessment of the high-priority technology needs of the criminal justice community, NIJ begins with the needs identified by the TWGs. Those needs are then refined in light of LECTAC's recommendations. NIJ also considers research and development being conducted elsewhere in finalizing its assessment.

Grant Solicitation Process

NIJ annually solicits applications for research and development leading to the introduction of new tools and technologies into criminal justice practice. Those solicitations are targeted to address the criminal justice high-priority technology needs identified in this document, within available funding. They are released through Grants.gov, the portal to find and apply for federal government grants. Proposals are reviewed by independent peer panels of scientists and engineers, principally from academic and government organizations, along with practitioners from local, state, tribal and federal agencies, including TWG representatives.

Based on the results of the peer reviews, NIJ program managers recommend individual proposals to the NIJ Director. Historically, approximately 8 percent of OST applicants receive awards.

NIJ awards grants to educational institutions, public agencies, nonprofit organizations, faith-based organizations, individuals, and for-profit organizations willing to waive their fees. Non-U.S. entities are not eligible for awards.

The Research, Development, Testing and Evaluation Process

The RDT&E process helps ensure that NIJ's research portfolios are aligned to best address the technology needs of the criminal justice community. The rigorous process has five phases:

- **Phase I: Determine technology needs.** Principally in partnership with TWGs and LECTAC, NIJ identifies criminal justice practitioners' functional requirements for new tools and technologies.

- **Phase II: Develop technology program plans to address those needs.** A multiyear research program is created to address the needs identified in phase I. One of the first steps is to determine whether products that meet those needs currently exist or whether they must be developed. If a solution is already available, phases II and III are not necessary, and NIJ moves directly to demonstration, testing and evaluation in phase IV. If solutions do not currently exist, they are solicited through annual, competitively awarded science and technology solicitations. TWG members help review the applications.

- **Phase III: Develop solutions.** Appropriate solicitations are developed. Grantees are selected through an open, competitive, peer-reviewed process, and grants are awarded. The grantee and the NIJ program manager then work collaboratively to develop the solutions.

- **Phase IV: Demonstrate, test, evaluate and adopt potential solutions into practice.** A potential solution is tested to determine how well it addresses the intended functional requirement. NIJ then works with first-adopting agencies to facilitate the introduction of the solution into practice. After adoption, the solution's impact on practice is evaluated. During the testing and evaluation process, performance standards and guides are developed as appropriate to ensure safety and effectiveness; not all new solutions will require the publication of new standards or guides.

- **Phase V: Build capacity and conduct outreach.** To ensure that the new tool or technology benefits practitioners, NIJ publishes guides and standards and provides technology assistance to second adopters.

The Research, Development, Testing and Evaluation Process

Phase I: Determine technology needs.

Technology Working Groups, LECTAC and others identify technology gaps

Phase II: Develop technology program plans.

Define requirements and identify solutions.

NIJ Program Managers maintain multiyear program plans for portfolio RDT&E.

Phase IV: Demonstrate, test, evaluate and adopt into practice.

Does it meet operational requirements?
No

NIJ tests and evaluates solutions.

Phase III: Develop solutions.

Yes — Are there existing solutions? — No

NIJ solicits applications to develop new solutions.

Independent peer review and selection of developer.

Yes

NIJ assists first adopters of new technology.

Is development successful?
Yes

Research and development.

Phase V: Build capacity and conduct outreach.

No

Does the solution improve practice, cost and public safety?
No / Yes

NIJ publishes guides and standards and provides technology assistance to practitioners

NIJ oversight and TWG review

Standards and Compliance Testing

NIJ's Office of Science and Technology administers a standards and compliance testing program to help ensure that the equipment used by criminal justice agencies will perform at a safe, dependable and effective level.

NIJ conducts two kinds of equipment testing: (1) standards-based testing and (2) comparative evaluations. In standards-based testing, products are tested in accordance with the performance standards developed by NIJ. In comparative evaluation, products are tested to determine how well they perform independent of a standard.

NIJ currently has 16 active standards with nine under development. For information on these standards, see http://www.ojp.usdoj. gov/nij/topics/technology/standards-testing/welcome.htm.

NIJ standards are voluntary performance standards. They do not specify a particular solution, but rather define what a potential solution must accomplish.

NIJ standards are an articulation of the criminal justice practitioner's operational needs and associated performance levels with regard to particular tools and technologies. They reflect the practical experiences of the community in the field articulated in such a way as to enable testing in a valid and consistently replicable manner. Many criminal justice agencies require compliance with NIJ standards as a condition for purchasing a piece of equipment.

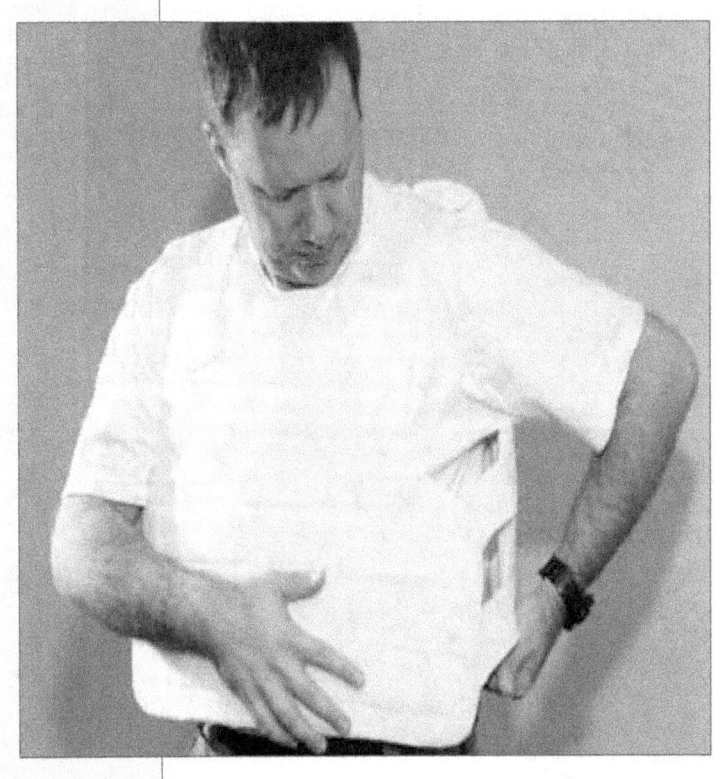

Once the need for a standard is determined through the RDT&E process, NIJ establishes a 20- to 25-member Special Technical Committee (STC) to develop it. An STC is a type of TWG made up of expert criminal justice practitioners with relevant experience supported by scientists, subject matter experts, test laboratory personnel and conformity assessment experts.

Practitioners on the committees also represent stakeholder organizations such as the International Association of Chiefs of Police and the Fraternal Order of Police.

During the development of a standard, NIJ conducts workshops with relevant vendors and manufacturers to give insight into the standard's evolving design and performance requirements. These workshops also inform the Special Technical Committee regarding the vendors' views of those requirements.

Prior to publication, a standard is made available for public review and comment.

Composition of a Standard

The following three interrelated documents together form the complete standard package:

Standard. The standard defines the minimum performance requirements that the equipment must meet and the test methods used to assess performance.

Conformity Assessment Requirements Document. The conformity assessment document details the process used to demonstrate that the equipment conforms to the standard. This document is written for certification bodies, testing laboratories and inspection bodies.

Selection and Application Guide. The selection and application guide describes the standard and conformity assessment requirements in nontechnical terms and provides guidance on selection, procurement, use, maintenance and disposal of the equipment.

Investing With Partners

Collaboration and coordination are core tenets of NIJ's science and technology investment strategy. Forming strategic partnerships with other agencies allows NIJ to leverage investments, avoid duplicating efforts and devote its resources to areas that offer the highest potential payoff for the criminal justice community.

NIJ shares responsibility with the U.S. Departments of Defense and Homeland Security for providing tools and technologies to deal with critical incidents resulting from natural or man-made disasters, including acts of terrorism. Terrorism is a crime, and law enforcement officers will often be among the first responders at the scene of an incident. In support of this mission, NIJ participates in overarching agreements on technology development and transfer with both departments.

Since the mid-1990s, NIJ has been a member of the Technical Support Working Group, the federal forum that identifies, prioritizes and coordinates interagency research and development activities for combating terrorism.

NIJ also has formal international agreements with the Australian National Institute of Forensic Science and the Israeli Ministry of Public Security. The Institute maintains informal relationships with the Royal Canadian Mounted Police and the U.K. Home Office Scientific Development Branch.

The 1401 Technology Transfer Program is an example of NIJ partnering. It is a collaboration among NIJ, the Department of Homeland Security's Science and Technology Directorate, and the Department of Defense's Office of the Assistant Secretary of Defense for Homeland Defense and America's Security Affairs to transfer military technology and equipment to support homeland security and public safety applications.

High-Priority Criminal Justice Technology Needs

The following pages summarize the high-priority needs for the criminal justice field in the area of technology. These needs are organized into five functional areas:

- Protecting the Public.

- Ensuring Officer Safety.

- Confirming the Guilty and Protecting the Innocent.

- Improving the Efficiency of Justice.

- Enabling Informed Decision-Making.

PROTECTING THE PUBLIC

- Assured means to continuously and accurately monitor the location and status of offenders under supervision in the community, including:

  - A noninvasive, assured method to continuously monitor an offender's substance abuse.

  - Within structures and outside in urban and rural environments.

  - Smaller, less obtrusive, more reliable and secure monitoring devices.

- Safer, more cost-effective aerial surveillance solutions to identify, locate and track illicit activities and to locate missing persons, particularly for application with small and rural agencies. Solutions must consider regulatory requirements.

- Improved, unobtrusive means to accurately detect a broad spectrum of contraband to preclude its introduction into public venues, including:

  - Academic institutions, including schools.

  - Mass transit.

- "Intelligent" surveillance solutions providing automated incident awareness and warnings in public venues, including:

  - Academic institutions, including schools.

  - Mass transit.

  - Sporting venues.

  - Shopping areas.

- Improved means to detect and respond to weapons concealed on an individual's body at a safe distance, including person-borne improvised explosive devices (IEDs).

- Improved, assured means to detect and effectively respond to vehicle-borne IEDs, which:

  - Are easily transportable.

  - Are rapidly and remotely deployable.

  - Cause minimal collateral effects.

- A means to remotely locate and track cooperative and uncooperative individuals inside buildings in hostage rescue and search situations.

- Improved characterization of currently available less-lethal devices and their health and safety effects, particularly on at-risk populations, leading to improved use-of-force protocols and to safer, more effective devices.

- New, safer, more effective less-lethal devices that:
  - Can better deter individuals from taking a prohibited action.
  - Can instantly incapacitate individuals for a specified period.
  - Are suitable for use on at-risk populations.

- Rapidly deployable, effective devices that can safely and remotely stop all types of vehicles under a variety of circumstances.

- Improved emergency response solutions, minimally including:
  - Accurate location of the incident.
  - Timely, optimized response.

Some Relevant Efforts

NIJ is funding GE Global Research (New York) to develop a "smart" closed-circuit television (CCTV) system that will be able to potentially anticipate criminal activity in public spaces, as well as detect it. In a related effort, NIJ is funding Temple University (Pennsylvania) to quantify the size and geographic extent of the impact of CCTV systems on reducing crime. Despite their proliferation, there is little empirical evidence on the effectiveness of CCTV systems on crime reduction.

NIJ is funding the Providence Plan (Rhode Island) to develop a geospatial application to help corrections, public safety and social service agencies better supervise and assist returning prisoners. The Providence Plan will design a Web-based tool using "open source" software that will enable users to conduct specialized queries of the locations of released prisoners, map the results and overlay results with other spatially enabled datasets.

NIJ is one of the largest sources of research into the physiological effects of conducted energy devices (CEDs), such as the Taser. NIJ-funded research has found that serious injuries or deaths associated with Taser deployment are very rare (approximately 0.3 percent of incidents) and that the device is safe and effective when used on healthy adults.

NIJ-funded evaluation research also suggests a significant reduction in injury to both the officer and detainee when CEDs are adopted by law enforcement agencies, if strong policies and sound training are in place. One of these research efforts was conducted by the Police Executive Research Forum.

ENSURING OFFICER SAFETY

- Confirming and fixing an individual's identity under all circumstances in a timely manner, including:

  - Identifying individuals from video and audio surveillance.

  - Positive identification and verification solutions, including:

    - Equipment and facility access control.

    - Positive identification of information technology systems users.

    - Incident scene access control.

  - An improved ability to effectively perform real-time, accurate identity checks across multiple jurisdictions and data systems.

  - An improved capability to collect and process biometric information at a crime scene in real time and remotely comparing it to information contained in criminal justice databases, including:

    - Capture and processing of latent finger and palm prints in a manner compatible with automated fingerprint information systems.

    - Iris scanning.

    - Facial recognition.

- Assured means to continuously and accurately monitor the location and status of individuals and equipment, including:

  - Law enforcement and corrections officers and personnel as well as inmates and detainees.

  - Health status of individuals, potentially:

    - Affordable, lightweight, physiological monitoring devices that can be embedded in clothing.

  - Within structures and outside in urban and rural environments.

- Improved solutions to assure communications under all circumstances, including:

  - A severely degraded terrestrial communications infrastructure resulting from a manmade or natural disaster.

  - An inadequate terrestrial communications infrastructure, such as may be found in some rural or tribal areas, but also in some parts of the urban law enforcement operating environment such as in buildings and subterranean areas.

- The availability of multiple, overlapping communications infrastructures with varying attributes.

- Cyber attacks (denial of service) against communications infrastructure critical systems.

■ Improved means to detect, isolate, locate and defeat the use of unauthorized wireless communications devices in all operating environments, including but not limited to, correctional environments. Solutions must consider regulatory requirements.

■ Improved, unobtrusive means to accurately detect a broad spectrum of contraband to

preclude its introduction into correctional and other operational environments, such as courthouses.

■ "Intelligent" surveillance solutions to monitor events in correctional and other operational environments and to identify and provide alerts on potentially dangerous situations prior to their occurring.

■ Improved all-hazards protection for law enforcement and corrections officers, including:

- Lighter weight, more flexible ballistic- and stab-resistant body armor systems that will stand up to environmental degradation and the normal "wear and tear" associated with continuous use.

- Cost-effective methods to reduce the heat-related stress associated with wearing existing body armor systems without compromising protection and mobility.

- Improved methods to ensure the continued performance of body armor systems, including:

  – More accurate means to measure deformations to the inside of a body armor system caused by impacts and perforations and their effect on the human body.

  – Accurate means to measure the protection afforded by in-service body armor systems.

- Tactile; reusable; and cut-, puncture- and pathogen-resistant gloves that provide full dexterity.

- Improved materials for everyday duty uniforms that are flame retardant, moisture proof, flexible and lightweight and that offer cut, puncture and pathogen resistance.

- A protective ensemble compatible with law enforcement tactical operations requirements that provides protection from biological agents, radiation exposure, and exposure to the toxic materials and gases associated with clandestine drug laboratories.

- A full-face respirator fully compatible with law enforcement tactical operations requirements.

- Improved robots and robotic tools that reduce the need for bomb technicians to deal directly with IEDs of all types.

- Proactive, targeted, location-based notification and distribution of alerts to officers.

Some Relevant Efforts

NIJ maintains and updates standards for bullet- and stab-resistant body armor. For more information on these standards, and the body armor models that comply with them, see http://www.justnet.org/Pages/Topic.aspx?opentopic=10&topic=10.

NIJ also has a number of standards under development aimed at ensuring officer safety, including one for retention holsters and restraints (e.g., handcuffs and plastic ties). In 2009, it completed development of a standard addressing the law enforcement responder's requirements for garment ensembles providing protection from chemical, radiological and nuclear hazards. That standard will be published in 2010. NIJ also has a standard under development for the protective ensembles worn by bomb technicians.

As part of its many related efforts to provide assured communications for criminal justice practitioners, NIJ has funded the Shared Spectrum Company (Virginia) to develop a spectrum management subsystem for cognitive radios. This subsystem will provide spectrum managers with flexible and adaptable tools to control a large number of cognitive radios. In addition, the subsystem facilitates the development and dissemination of a wide range of spectrum access and priority rules.

CONFIRMING THE GUILTY AND PROTECTING THE INNOCENT

■ Improved capability to expand the information that can be extracted from traditional types of forensic evidence and to quantify its evidentiary value, including:

• Identification or characterization of:

– Biological markers that may reveal more information about the source of biological evidence.

– New substances or chemical constituents of forensic importance.

• Improved tools for examining aged, degraded, limited, damaged, inhibited or otherwise compromised DNA evidence.

• Tools to expand the utility of Y-chromosome and mitochondrial DNA.

• Tools that provide a quantitative measure/ statistical evaluation of forensic comparisons, including:

– Impression evidence, such as friction ridge analysis, questioned document examination, firearms and toolmarks examination, and shoeprint/tire tread examination.

• Physical separation of cells or components in mixtures from two or more individuals or sources, including:

– Sperm.

■ Improved capability to use and process digital evidence, including:

• Tools to investigate the use of peer-to-peer technologies used to facilitate criminal activity, such as distribution of contraband, that address decentralized and unstructured peer-to-peer network protocols.

• Tools that can recover system files, operating system information, applications, deleted files and unallocated space from small-scale mobile devices, such as cell phones and personal digital assistants.

• Full data imaging solutions for networks and network-attached or -connected devices addressing:

– Redundant Array of Independent Disks (RAID).

– Wireless network devices, including routers, gateways, network interface cards, repeaters, switches, hubs and wirelessly connected external digital media.

– Network data storage devices that are either directly connected or connected by a computer to the network.

■ Improved means to verify the veracity of interviews.

■ Improved ability to effectively perform real-time, accurate identity checks across multiple jurisdictions and data systems, including:

• Improved solutions to automatically determine that related entries in multiple databases that contain varying or inexact details are attributable to the same person.

• Improved, more accurate information extraction from biometric data.

■ Fundamental research to improve understanding of the accuracy, reliability and measurement validity of the forensic science disciplines, including:

• Studies that examine the degree of accuracy and reliability of methods used by forensic scientists.

• Research to further a full understanding of quantifiable measures of uncertainty in the conclusions of forensic analyses, regardless of the sources of uncertainty.

• Research to develop new approaches to forensic analysis, including quantitation of analyses that are currently qualitative in nature.

• Research to examine human factors affecting forensic practice, including potential systemic errors.

Some Relevant Efforts

In the field of forensics, NIJ-funded research led to the development of "mini-STRs" that can generate a DNA profile from aged, degraded or damaged samples such as skeletal remains. This has greatly expanded the power of DNA technology to identify the guilty, exonerate the innocent and identify the missing.

NIJ is also the largest funding source for research to improve the understanding of the accuracy, reliability and measurement validity of the forensic science disciplines. It has long funded this work in the area of impression evidence. NIJ is currently funding research at the University of California, Los Angeles, to examine how the visual complexity of a fingerprint and the examiner's perception, judgment and decision-making processes affect the error rates of latent fingerprint examination.

IMPROVING THE EFFICIENCY OF JUSTICE

- "Intelligent" decision support systems, including:

  - Optimizing sentencing (e.g., institutionalization, probation, parole, therapy, electronic monitoring or treatment), taking into account cost, safety and recidivism issues.

  - Optimizing the way in which law enforcement agencies organize and deploy their resources, to include: patrol district, precinct and beat designs; fleet maintenance; and management and manpower scheduling.

  - Optimizing the way in which law enforcement and corrections agencies employ new technologies, such as automated vehicle locators, smart sensors, wireless mobile networks, and knowledge management, in patrol and response operations.

- Improved information and data systems that link an individual's records and citations across various criminal justice databases from the time of entry into the criminal justice system.

- Secure Web applications (services) that facilitate effective cross-jurisdiction information and data sharing and exchange. Solutions must consider the Justice Reference Architecture.

- Immersive technologies to effectively train criminal justice practitioners, optimally at their stations, focusing on:

  - Low probability, but high consequence events (critical incidents) such as an active shooter in a school.

- Devices providing multilingual speech translation capabilities for criminal justice applications, including:

  - Voice.

  - Speech-to-text/text-to-speech.

- Reliable and widely applicable tools and technologies that allow faster, cheaper and less labor-intensive identification, collection, preservation and analysis of forensic evidence of all kinds and the reduction of existing case backlogs, including cold and missing person cases. These include:

Some Relevant Efforts

NIJ funded the development, and funds the operation, of the National Missing and Unidentified Persons System (NamUs). NamUs is a clearinghouse for missing persons and unidentified decedent records. It is a free online system that can be searched by medical examiners, coroners, law enforcement officials and the general public to solve these cases. When a new missing person or unidentified decedent case is entered into NamUs, the system automatically performs cross-matching comparisons between the databases, searching for matches or similarities between cases.

NIJ is also funding development of the Forensic Information Data Exchange (FIDEX). FIDEX provides a bridge to connect the various databases used by law enforcement, crime laboratories and the courts to improve the efficiency with which cases are processed. Among its capabilities FIDEX enables the sharing of data between a police department records management system or evidence management system with a crime laboratory's information management system. It also enables the sharing of disposition information issued by local law enforcement and the prosecutors' offices with crime laboratories.

- Improved laboratory information management systems.

- Improved automated forensic analysis.

- Improved quality assurance processes.

- Improved screening methods for use at crime scenes and in the laboratory to rapidly and accurately determine the evidentiary value of biological materials.

- Improved methods to rapidly identify and collect biological evidentiary samples at a crime scene.

- Improved tools for preserving biological evidence.

- Improved methods for DNA extraction, analysis and interpretation (including the use of expert systems for data analysis).

- Improved solutions to address the need for increased data storage capacity to archive large-volume datasets generated in computer forensic examinations.

- Improved solutions for extracting specific data subsets that correspond to specific files from larger datasets during analysis of unallocated space on a digital media device.

- Improved solutions to automatically determine that related entries in multiple databases that may contain differing kinds of data and have varying or inexact details are attributable to the same person, including missing persons.

ENABLING INFORMED DECISION-MAKING

- Effective and instantaneous, user-transparent, operable and interoperable voice, data, and multimedia communications under all circumstances, including:

  - Wired or wireless networks.

  - Vehicular (including aerial) or foot-mobile.

  - In areas with limited or no terrestrial communications infrastructure.

  - At the dynamic data rates needed for effective criminal justice operations, including video transfer.

  - Mobile hybrid technology for wireless broadband data that seamlessly locates the best route and operational band under any circumstances, across multiple networks with varying attributes.

  - Advanced in-building communications that do not rely on pre-existing systems.

- Improved spatial analysis tools and technologies, including:

  - Improved data management and analytical tools compatible with the mobile and handheld computing devices used by criminal justice agencies.

  - Tools to analyze the geographical linkages of relationships among people, groups and organizations of interest to criminal justice agencies.

  - Exploratory spatial and temporal data analysis visualization tools that examine data in new and unique ways or that extend current capabilities of exploiting crime-related databases.

  - Mapping tools that make geo-coded data available and compatible with the mobile and handheld computing devices used by law enforcement.

  - Tools providing 3-D geo-coding and mapping for large buildings, including those with no electronic computer-aided design files.

  - Tools that identify and extract relationships hidden in large, complex law enforcement agency datasets and implement crime theories in a geographic information system environment.

Some Relevant Efforts

NIJ has made a significant investment in development of cognitive and software-defined radio (SDR) and antenna technology for law enforcement application. It is, for example, funding the University of Texas at Dallas to implement a public safety SDR code in the Texas Instruments' commercial Digital Radio Processor. It is also funding Utah State University to develop an integrated, reconfigurable antenna for handheld SDRs using nanoelectro-mechanical systems (NEMS) technology. The proposed antenna will be compatible with multiband/mode communications systems operating within the public safety radio bands of 150, 400, 700, 800 and 4900 MHz.

NIJ is the largest funding source for development of geospatial technologies for law enforcement application. It is funding Towson University (Maryland) to develop a new mathematical approach to geographic profiling that incorporates geographic features that affect both the selection of crime sites as well as geographic and demographic features that influence the distribution of offender anchor points. The software will be available at no cost to law enforcement agencies and researchers.

NIJ is funding the Research Triangle Institute (North Carolina) to create a software toolkit for processing and analyzing 911 calls for service to develop a clearer picture of criminal and homeland security threats. This effort will develop automated processes for identifying changes in small geographic areas, linking incidents across time and space, and associating seemingly unrelated 911 calls that are actually part of a larger sequence of events.

■ Affordable and open-source tools that can analyze data across databases and domains received through federated queries to create informed information-led intelligence.

■ "Intelligent" automated solutions that can predict and deter potential criminal activity by correlating patterns of behavior and anomalies in that behavior from multiple data sources, including:

- Databases.
- Real-time video and audio surveillance.
- Real-time geospatial tracking data.
- Social networking.

■ Better solutions to the effective integration and management of sensor systems in law enforcement command and control systems.

- Automated case management and communications systems that can be used by officers and offenders to track compliance with conditions of release and prompt necessary action.

- Proactive, targeted, location-based notification and distribution of alerts to officers.

NIJ Resources

- http://www.DNA.gov. This Web site is a one-stop resource for information about the President's DNA Initiative, including grant and training opportunities.

- http://www.JUSTNET.org. The Justice Technology Information Network (JUST-NET), created in 1995, acts as a gateway to the products and services of the NLECTC system and to other technology information and services of interest to the law enforcement and corrections communities.

- http://www.ncjrs.gov. The National Criminal Justice Reference Service (NCJRS) is a federally funded resource offering justice and substance abuse information to support research, policy and program development worldwide.

- http://www.namus.gov. The National Missing and Unidentified Persons System (NamUs) is the first national online repository for missing persons records and unidentified decedent cases. NIJ launched NamUs in July 2007.

- http://www.less-lethal.org. This Web site was created by the Less Lethal Working Group to assist local, state and federal law enforcement agencies in developing, implementing and enhancing policies governing the use of less-lethal (commonly referred to as nonlethal) technologies.